ROASTING

MARKS &
SPENCER

ROASTING

PETER SWANN

Marks and Spencer p.l.c.
PO Box 3339
Chester CH99 9QS

T40/8283/0212B

www.marksandspencer.com

ISBN: 1-84461-293-7

Printed in China

Produced by the Bridgewater Book Company Ltd

Main Photographer: Laurie Evans

Main Home Economist: Annie Rigg

Notes for the Reader

This book uses both metric and imperial measurements. Follow the same units of measurement throughout; do not mix metric and imperial. All spoon measurements are level: teaspoons are assumed to be 5 ml, and tablespoons are assumed to be 15 ml. Unless otherwise stated, milk is assumed to be full fat, eggs and individual vegetables such as potatoes are medium and pepper is freshly ground black pepper. Recipes using raw or very lightly cooked eggs should be avoided by infants, the elderly, pregnant women, convalescents and anyone suffering from an illness. The times given are an approximate guide only. Preparation times differ according to the techniques used by different people and the cooking times may also vary from those given. Optional ingredients, variations or serving suggestions have not been included in the calculations.

Picture acknowledgments
The Bridgewater Book Company would like to thank the following for permission to reproduce copyright material: Corbis Images, pages 6, 8, 30, 52; Getty Images, page 74.

CONTENTS

INTRODUCTION 6

FROM THE CARVERY 8

THE GAMEKEEPER'S CHOICE 30

THE OCEAN SELECTION 52

FRESH FROM THE GARDEN 74

INDEX 96

Roasting is the technique of cooking in radiant heat and it can be used for a wide variety of ingredients, including meat, poultry, game, fish and vegetables. All the recipes in this book have been tested in conventional ovens, so you won't have to worry about buying expensive gadgets, such as rotisseries for spit roasting, and they work just as successfully whatever fuel you are using in your kitchen.

It's unlikely you will need to rush out and buy any other extra equipment either. It's worth having a couple of good-quality, heavy roasting tins – a larger one for a turkey or a rib of beef and a smaller one in which vegetables and fish fillets can fit snugly. If the tin is too large for its contents, fat will spit messily all over the inside of the oven. If it's too small, cooking may be uneven and fat can spill over the sides, risking a dangerous fire. If the tins are heavyweight, they ensure even cooking and last a lifetime.

INTRODUCTION

A good, flexible carving knife with a blade 30–35 cm/12–14 in long is also essential and a knife sharpener will keep it in good condition. Always allow roast meat to stand, tented with foil to keep it warm, for 10–20 minutes after removing it from the oven. This evens out the residual heat and stabilizes the texture, making it easier to carve into neat slices. A carving fork is not essential, but is a worthwhile safety feature.

Meat is the most popular ingredient for roasting and the traditional favourite for family meals. While the classic Sunday roast fell out of favour for a time, it is enjoying renewed popularity, especially now that leaner cuts are widely available. However, do bear in mind that some fat is necessary to keep the meat moist during cooking and to intensify the flavour.

Lamb is the perfect choice for spring, although it is available throughout the year. Leg is ideal if you are feeding a number of guests and rack of lamb looks attractive as well as being easy to carve. Shoulder is often said to have the sweetest meat, but it is more awkward to carve. However, you can buy it boned and rolled. Lamb is usually served while still pink in the middle.

It is not a coincidence that the French nicknamed the British *les rosbifs* as beef has been a favourite roast for centuries. For oven roasting, larger joints are best, particularly rib.

PART ONE
FROM THE CARVERY

Fillet may be roasted for special occasions, but it must be well larded and basted frequently during cooking. Slightly tougher cuts, such as brisket and topside, are suitable for the slower method of pot roasting.

There are many different cuts of pork in a wide range of sizes that are suitable for roasting Perhaps the most popular is boned and rolled loin, as it is very tender and easy to carve, while leg is an economical buy if you are feeding a large number of people. Unlike lamb and beef, pork must always be well cooked. Check by piercing it with a skewer to see if the juices run clear. Alternatively, use a meat thermometer. It is done when this registers 80°C/176°F.

ROAST BEEF

SERVES 8

1 prime rib of beef joint, weighing 2.7 kg/6 lb

2 tsp dry English mustard

3 tbsp plain flour

300 ml/10 fl oz red wine

300 ml/10 fl oz beef stock

2 tsp Worcestershire sauce (optional)

salt and pepper

Yorkshire pudding, to serve

Preheat the oven to 230°C/450°F/Gas Mark 8.

Season the meat to taste with salt and pepper. Rub in the mustard and 1 tablespoon of the flour.

Place the meat in a roasting tin large enough to hold it comfortably and roast in the oven for 15 minutes. Reduce the temperature to 190°C/375°F/Gas Mark 5 and cook for 15 minutes per 450 g/1 lb, plus 15 minutes (1 3/4 hours for this joint) for rare beef or 20 minutes per 450 g/1 lb, plus 20 minutes (2 hours 20 minutes) for medium beef. Baste the meat from time to time to keep it moist, and if the tin becomes too dry, add a little stock or red wine.

Remove the meat from the oven and place on a warmed serving plate, cover with foil and leave in a warm place for 10–15 minutes.

To make the gravy, pour off most of the fat from the tin (reserve it for cooking the Yorkshire pudding), leaving behind the meat juices and the sediment. Place the tin on the hob over a medium heat and scrape all the sediment from the base of the tin. Sprinkle in the remaining flour and quickly mix it into the juices with a small whisk. When you have a smooth paste, gradually add the wine and most of the stock, whisking constantly. Bring to the boil, then reduce the heat to a gentle simmer and cook for 2–3 minutes. Season to taste with salt and pepper and add the remaining stock, if needed, and a little Worcestershire sauce, if you like.

When ready to serve, carve the meat into slices and serve on warmed plates. Pour the gravy into a warmed jug and take direct to the table. Serve with Yorkshire pudding.

ROAST BEEF IS A DIFFICULT ROAST TO GET RIGHT BECAUSE, UNLIKE MOST OTHER MEATS, HOW WELL COOKED THE MEAT SHOULD BE IS VERY MUCH A CASE OF PERSONAL PREFERENCE. THE BEST ROAST BEEF IS A RIB COOKED ON THE BONE, BUT THIS MUST BE A GOOD SIZE.

BEEF POT ROAST WITH POTATOES AND DILL

SERVES 6

2¹/₂ tbsp plain flour

1 tsp salt

¹/₄ tsp pepper

1 rolled brisket joint, weighing 1.6 kg/3 lb 8 oz

2 tbsp vegetable oil

2 tbsp butter

1 onion, finely chopped

2 celery sticks, diced

2 carrots, peeled and diced

1 tsp dill seed

1 tsp dried thyme or oregano

350 ml/12 fl oz red wine

150–225 ml/5–8 fl oz beef stock

4–5 potatoes, cut into large chunks and boiled until just tender

2 tbsp chopped fresh dill, to serve

Preheat the oven to 140°C/275°F/Gas Mark 1.

Mix 2 tablespoons of the flour with the salt and pepper in a shallow dish. Dip the meat to coat. Heat the oil in a flameproof casserole and brown the meat all over. Transfer to a plate.

Add half the butter to the casserole and cook the onion, celery, carrots, dill seed and thyme for 5 minutes. Return the meat and juices to the casserole.

Pour in the wine and enough stock to reach one-third of the way up the meat. Bring to the boil, cover and cook in the oven for 3 hours, turning the meat every 30 minutes. After it has been cooking for 2 hours, add the potatoes and more stock if necessary.

When ready, transfer the meat and vegetables to a warmed serving dish. Strain the cooking liquid into a saucepan.

Mix the remaining butter and flour to a paste. Bring the cooking liquid to the boil. Whisk in small pieces of the flour and butter paste, whisking constantly until the sauce is smooth. Pour the sauce over the meat and vegetables. Sprinkle with the fresh dill to serve.

WHEN USING A FLOUR AND BUTTER PASTE, ALSO KNOWN AS BEURRE MANIÉ, TO THICKEN A SAUCE OR GRAVY, WHISK IT INTO THE SAUCE IN SMALL PIECES, MAKING SURE EACH PIECE HAS BEEN BLENDED IN BEFORE ADDING THE NEXT.

RACK OF LAMB

SERVES 2

1 trimmed rack of lamb,
weighing 250–300 g/
9–10½ oz

1 garlic clove, crushed

150 ml/5 fl oz red wine

1 fresh rosemary sprig,
crushed to release
the flavour

1 tbsp olive oil

150 ml/5 fl oz lamb stock

2 tbsp redcurrant jelly

salt and pepper

Mint sauce

Bunch fresh mint leaves

2 tsp caster sugar

2 tbsp water

2 tbsp white wine vinegar

Place the rack of lamb in a non-metallic bowl and rub all over with the garlic. Pour over the wine and place the rosemary sprig on top. Cover and leave to marinate in the refrigerator for 3 hours or overnight if possible.

Preheat the oven to 220°C/425°F/Gas Mark 7. Remove the lamb from the marinade, reserving the marinade. Pat the meat dry with kitchen paper and season well with salt and pepper. Place it in a small roasting tin, drizzle with the oil and roast for 15–20 minutes, depending on whether you like your meat pink or medium. Remove the lamb from the oven and leave to rest, covered with foil, in a warm place for 5 minutes.

Meanwhile, pour the reserved marinade into a small saucepan, bring to the boil over a medium heat and bubble gently for 2–3 minutes. Add the stock and redcurrant jelly and simmer, stirring, until the mixture is syrupy.

To make the Mint Sauce, chop the fresh mint leaves and mix together with the sugar in a small bowl. Add the boiling water and stir to dissolve the sugar. Add the white wine vinegar and leave to stand for 30 minutes before serving with the lamb.

Carve the lamb into cutlets and serve on warmed plates with the sauce spooned over the top. Serve the Mint Sauce separately.

Lamb is best in spring, from Easter onwards, when it is at its sweetest and most succulent. Rosemary and garlic are traditional flavourings and a gravy made with red wine and redcurrant jelly is divine. Fresh mint for sauce is also at its best around this time. Rack of lamb is an impressive dish for entertaining, too. Just double or treble the ingredients, depending on the number of guests.

POT ROASTED LEG OF LAMB

SERVES 4

1 leg of lamb, weighing
1.6 kg/3 lb 8 oz

3–4 fresh rosemary sprigs

115 g/4 oz streaky
bacon rashers

4 tbsp olive oil

2–3 garlic cloves, crushed

2 onions, sliced

2 carrots, sliced

2 celery sticks, sliced

300 ml/10 fl oz dry
white wine

1 tbsp tomato purée

300 ml/10 fl oz lamb or
chicken stock

3 medium tomatoes,
peeled, quartered and
deseeded

1 tbsp chopped
fresh parsley

1 tbsp chopped fresh
oregano or marjoram

salt and pepper

fresh rosemary sprigs,
to garnish

Wipe the lamb all over with kitchen paper, trim off any excess fat and season to taste with salt and pepper, rubbing well in. Lay the sprigs of rosemary over the lamb, cover evenly with the bacon rashers and tie securely in place with kitchen string.

Heat the oil in a frying pan and fry the lamb over a medium heat for 10 minutes, turning several times. Remove from the pan.

Preheat the oven to 160°C/325°F/Gas Mark 3. Transfer the oil from the frying pan to a large flameproof casserole and cook the garlic and onions for 3–4 minutes until the onions are beginning to soften. Add the carrots and celery and cook for a further few minutes.

Lay the lamb on top of the vegetables and press down to partly submerge. Pour the wine over the lamb, add the tomato purée and simmer for 3–4 minutes. Add the stock, tomatoes and herbs and season to taste with salt and pepper. Return to the boil for a further 3–4 minutes.

Cover the casserole tightly and cook in the oven for 2–2½ hours until very tender.

Remove the lamb from the casserole and, if you like, remove the bacon and herbs together with the string. Keep the lamb warm. Strain the juices, skimming off any excess fat, and serve in a jug. The vegetables may be put around the joint or in a dish. Garnish with sprigs of rosemary.

THIS DISH FROM THE ABRUZZI REGION OF ITALY USES A SLOW COOKING METHOD. THE MEAT ABSORBS THE FLAVOURINGS AND BECOMES VERY TENDER.

ROAST LAMB WITH ORZO

SERVES 4

1 boned leg or shoulder
of lamb, weighing about
750 g/1 lb 10 oz

1/2 lemon, thinly sliced

1 tbsp chopped
fresh oregano

4 large garlic cloves,
2 finely chopped and
2 thinly sliced

800 g/1 lb 12 oz canned
chopped tomatoes

150 ml/5 fl oz cold water

pinch of sugar

1 bay leaf

2 tbsp olive oil

150 ml/5 fl oz boiling
water

225 g/8 oz orzo or short-
grain rice

salt and pepper

Preheat the oven to 180°C/350°F/Gas Mark 4.

Untie the lamb and open out. Place the lemon slices along the middle and sprinkle over half the oregano, the chopped garlic and salt and pepper to taste. Roll up the meat and tie with string. Cut slits in the lamb and insert the garlic slices.

Weigh the meat and calculate the cooking time, allowing 25 minutes per 450 g/1 lb, plus 25 minutes.

Put the tomatoes and their can juices, cold water, remaining oregano, the sugar and bay leaf in a large roasting tin. Place the lamb on top, drizzle over the oil and season to taste with salt and pepper.

Roast the lamb in the oven for the calculated cooking time. Fifteen minutes before the lamb will be cooked, stir the boiling water and orzo into the tomatoes. Add a little extra water if the sauce seems too thick. Return to the oven for a further 15 minutes, until the lamb and orzo are tender and the tomatoes are reduced to a thick sauce.

To serve, carve the lamb into slices and serve hot with the orzo and tomato sauce.

ORZO IS A VERY SMALL FORM OF PASTA THAT LOOKS LIKE FLAT WHEAT GRAINS. IT IS USED IN SOUP AND MEAT DISHES AND SERVED AS AN ACCOMPANIMENT. IN THIS RECIPE IT IS BAKED WITH LAMB AND ABSORBS THE MEAT JUICES, GIVING IT THE MOST WONDERFUL FLAVOUR. THIS IS AN IMMENSELY POPULAR DISH IN GREECE, WHERE IT IS ALSO MADE WITH KID AND BEEF.

ROAST LAMB WITH
ROSEMARY AND MARSALA

SERVES 6

1 leg of lamb, weighing
1.8 kg/4 lb

2 garlic cloves,
thinly sliced

2 tbsp fresh or dried
rosemary leaves

8 tbsp olive oil

900 g/2 lb potatoes, cut
into 2.5-cm/1-inch cubes

6 fresh sage
leaves, chopped

150 ml/5 fl oz Marsala

salt and pepper

Preheat the oven to 220°C/425°F/Gas Mark 7.

Use a small, sharp knife to make incisions all over the lamb, opening them out slightly to make little pockets. Insert the garlic slices and about half the rosemary leaves in the pockets.

Place the lamb in a roasting tin and spoon over half the oil. Roast in the oven for 15 minutes.

Reduce the oven temperature to 180°C/350°F/Gas Mark 4. Remove the lamb from the oven and season to taste with salt and pepper.

Turn the lamb over, return it to the oven and roast for a further hour.

Meanwhile, spread out the cubed potatoes in a second roasting tin, pour the remaining oil over them and toss to coat. Sprinkle with the remaining rosemary and the sage. Place the potatoes in the oven with the lamb and roast for 40 minutes.

Remove the lamb from the oven, turn it over and pour over the Marsala. Return it to the oven with the potatoes and cook for a further 15 minutes. Transfer the lamb to a carving board and cover with foil. Place the roasting tin over a high heat and bring the juices to the boil. Continue to boil until thickened and syrupy. Strain into a warmed sauce boat or jug.

Carve the lamb into slices and serve with the potatoes and sauce.

SERVING TENDER SPRING LAMB ON EASTER SUNDAY TO CELEBRATE THE END OF THE LENTEN FAST IS TRADITIONAL THROUGHOUT THE MEDITERRANEAN, NOT LEAST IN ITALY WHERE THIS DISH ORIGINATES.

ROAST GAMMON

SERVES 6

1 boneless gammon joint,
weighing 1.3 kg/3 lb,
pre-soaked if necessary

2 tbsp Dijon mustard

85 g/3 oz demerara sugar

¹/₂ tsp ground cinnamon

¹/₂ tsp ground ginger

18 whole cloves

Cumberland sauce

2 Seville oranges, halved

4 tbsp redcurrant jelly

4 tbsp port

1 tsp mustard

salt and pepper

Place the joint in a large saucepan, cover with cold water and gradually bring to the boil over a low heat. Cover and simmer very gently for 1 hour. Preheat the oven to 200°C/400°F/Gas Mark 6.

Remove the gammon from the saucepan and drain. Remove the rind from the gammon and discard. Score the fat into a diamond-shaped pattern with a sharp knife.

Spread the mustard over the fat. Mix the sugar and ground spices together on a plate and roll the gammon in it, pressing down to coat evenly.

Stud the diamond shapes with cloves and place the joint in a roasting tin. Roast in the oven for 20 minutes until the glaze is a rich golden colour.

To serve hot, cover with foil and leave to stand for 20 minutes before carving. If the gammon is to be served cold, it can be cooked a day ahead. Serve with Cumberland Sauce.

Using a citrus zester, remove the zest of the oranges. Place the redcurrant jelly, port and mustard in a small saucepan and heat gently until the jelly has melted. Squeeze the juice from the oranges into the saucepan. Add the orange zest and season to taste with salt and pepper. Serve cold with gammon. The sauce can be kept in a screw-top jar in the refrigerator for up to 2 weeks.

ROAST GAMMON OR HAM HAS LONG BEEN A FAVOURITE CHOICE FOR SUNDAY LUNCH AND FOR BOXING DAY DINNER. BOTH GAMMON AND HAM ARE SALTED, EITHER BY SALT CURING OR SOAKING IN BRINE, AND SOME VARIETIES, SUCH AS YORK HAM, MAY BE SMOKED. SOME JOINTS MAY NEED TO BE SOAKED IN COLD WATER FOR 2 HOURS OR OVERNIGHT TO REDUCE THE SALTINESS (CHECK WITH YOUR BUTCHER, OR ON THE PACKAGING, TO SEE IF IT HAS BEEN PRE-SOAKED). THE SWEET GLAZE OF HAMS, OR THE SERVING OF A SWEET ACCOMPANIMENT SUCH AS CUMBERLAND SAUCE, IS TO COUNTERACT THE SALT.

SLOW·ROASTED PORK

SERVES 6

1 piece of loin of pork, weighing 1.6 kg/3 lb 8 oz, boned and rolled

4 garlic cloves, thinly sliced lengthways

1 1/2 tsp finely chopped fennel fronds or 1/2 tsp dried fennel

4 cloves

300 ml/10 fl oz dry white wine

300 ml/10 fl oz water

salt and pepper

Preheat the oven to 150°C/300°F/Gas Mark 2.

Use a small, sharp knife to make incisions all over the pork, opening them out slightly to make little pockets. Place the garlic slices in a small sieve and rinse under cold running water to moisten. Spread out the fennel on a saucer and roll the garlic slices in it to coat. Slide the garlic slices and the cloves into the pockets in the pork. Season the meat all over to taste with salt and pepper.

Place the pork in a large ovenproof dish or roasting tin. Pour in the wine and water. Cook in the oven, basting the meat occasionally, for 2 1/2–2 3/4 hours, until the pork is tender but still quite moist.

If you are serving the pork hot, transfer it to a carving board, cover with foil and leave to rest before cutting it into slices. If you are serving it cold, leave it to cool completely in the cooking juices before removing and slicing.

READY-PREPARED BONED AND ROLLED LOIN OF PORK IS AVAILABLE FROM SUPERMARKETS AND BUTCHERS. OR YOU CAN ASK YOUR BUTCHER TO PREPARE ONE ESPECIALLY FOR YOU.

ROAST PORK WITH CRACKLING

SERVES 4

1 piece of loin of pork, weighing 1 kg/2 lb 4 oz, boned and the rind removed and reserved

2 tbsp mustard

salt and pepper

Apple Sauce (see Accompaniment), to serve

Gravy

1 tbsp flour

300 ml/10 fl oz cider, apple juice or chicken stock

Preheat the oven to 200°C/400°F/Gas Mark 6.

Score the pork rind thoroughly with a sharp knife and sprinkle with salt. Place it on a wire rack on a baking tray and roast in the oven for 30–40 minutes until the crackling is golden brown and crisp. This can be cooked in advance, leaving room in the oven for roast potatoes.

Season the pork well with salt and pepper and spread the fat with the mustard. Place in a roasting tin and roast in the centre of the oven for 20 minutes. Reduce the oven temperature to 190°C/375°F/Gas Mark 5 and cook for a further 50–60 minutes until the meat is a good colour and the juices run clear when it is pierced with a skewer.

ROAST PORK CAN BE DELICIOUS OR DISAPPOINTING. IT IS ALL TO DO WITH THE QUALITY OF THE PORK AND WHETHER THE FAT WILL 'CRACKLE' PROPERLY. THE CRACKLING IS ALL IMPORTANT. IT IS THE FAVOURITE PART OF THE JOINT, AND UNLESS IT IS CRISP AND CRUNCHY, THE WHOLE MEAL WILL BE A DISAPPOINTMENT. THE BEST JOINTS OF PORK FOR ROASTING ARE THE LEG AND THE LOIN. CHOOSE THE LEG IF YOU ARE CATERING FOR LARGE NUMBERS, ALTHOUGH THE LOIN, WHICH CAN BE BOUGHT IN SMALLER SIZES, IS THE BEST FOR CRACKLING.

Remove the meat from the oven and place on a warmed serving plate, cover with foil and leave in a warm place.

To make the gravy, pour off most of the fat from the roasting tin, leaving the meat juices and the sediment. Place the tin over a low heat. Sprinkle in the flour, whisking well. Cook the paste for a couple of minutes, then add the cider a little at a time until you have a smooth gravy. Boil for 2–3 minutes until it is the required consistency. Season well with salt and pepper and pour into a warmed serving jug.

Carve the pork into slices and serve on warmed plates with pieces of the crackling and the gravy. Accompany with Apple Sauce.

Apple Sauce

Peel, core and slice 450 g/1 lb Bramley apples into a medium saucepan. Add 3 tablespoons water and 15 g/½ oz caster sugar and cook over a low heat for 10 minutes, stirring occasionally. A little ground cinnamon can be added, as can 15 g/½ oz butter, if you like. Beat well until the sauce is thick and smooth – use a hand mixer for a really smooth finish.

PORK WITH SWEET PEPPERS

SERVES 4–6

1 piece of pork shoulder, weighing 900 g/2 lb, boned and trimmed, but left in 1 piece

225 ml/8 fl oz dry white wine

6 garlic cloves, crushed

2 dried ancho or pasilla chillies

about 4 tbsp olive oil

2 large onions, chopped

4 red or green peppers, or a mixture, grilled, peeled, deseeded and sliced

1/2 tsp hot paprika

800 g/1 lb 12 oz canned chopped tomatoes

2 fresh thyme sprigs

2 fresh parsley sprigs

salt and pepper

Place the pork in a non-metallic bowl. Pour over the wine and add 4 of the garlic cloves. Cover with clingfilm and leave to marinate in the refrigerator for at least 8 hours.

Put the chillies in a heatproof bowl and pour over enough boiling water to cover. Leave for 20 minutes to soften, then deseed and chop. Set them aside.

Preheat the oven to 160°C/325°F/Gas Mark 3.

Heat 4 tablespoons of oil in a large, heavy-based flameproof casserole over a medium-high heat. Add the onions and fry for 3 minutes, then add the remaining garlic, chopped chillies, pepper slices and paprika and fry for a further 2 minutes until the onions are soft, but not brown. Use a slotted spoon to transfer the mixture to a plate, leaving as much oil as possible in the base of the casserole.

Drain the pork, reserving the marinade, and pat dry. Add the pork to the casserole, and fry until brown on both sides.

Return the onion mixture to the casserole with the pork and stir in the reserved marinade, tomatoes and their can juices, the herbs and salt and pepper to taste. Bring to the boil, scraping any glazed bits from the base of the pan. Cover, transfer the casserole to the oven and cook for 1 hour, or until the pork is tender. If the juices are too thin, remove the pork from the casserole and keep warm. Put the casserole over a high heat and let the juices bubble until reduced.

Taste and adjust the seasoning. Cut the pork into serving pieces and serve with the peppers and sauce from the casserole.

COOKING 'AL CHILINDRÓN' IS POPULAR THROUGHOUT SPAIN, BUT IT WAS ORIGINALLY FROM THE NORTHERN REGIONS OF NAVARRE AND ARAGON, WHERE THE RUGGED CONDITIONS DEMANDED HEARTY, FULL-FLAVOURED DISHES. THE DRIED CHILLIES IN THIS RECIPE PROVIDE A CLOSE-TO-AUTHENTIC FIERY FLAVOUR, SO FOR A MILDER DISH, USE DRIED ÑORA CHILLIES. YOU NEED TO MARINATE THE PORK FOR AT LEAST 8 HOURS, PREFERABLY OVERNIGHT.

It is hard to believe that a couple of generations ago, roast chicken was a rare and expensive treat reserved for special occasions. Modern farming methods have made it much less costly and more routine, often at the expense of both flavour and texture. However, good-quality, free-range chicken still has that special magic and remains a family favourite. Poussins, also known as spring chicken, are popular and fun to serve, each bird providing a single portion.

Turkey has been the first choice for feeding large gatherings for a long time and that Dickensian favourite, goose, while rather expensive, has made a great comeback in recent years. Duckling, too, has become very fashionable, having moved on from its bistro guise in sticky orange sauce. It's certainly worth trying the clever boned and stuffed recipe in this chapter, which provides a delicious and surprisingly substantial feast.

PART TWO
THE GAMEKEEPER'S CHOICE

All kinds of game are now much more widely available, as venison and feathered game are increasingly farmed. Fresh game remains a seasonal treat, but it is often available frozen all year round. Like poultry, frozen game should be thoroughly thawed before cooking. These days, most game is sold oven-ready, so you don't have to endure the time-consuming, tricky and messy tasks of plucking and drawing it yourself.

Roast pheasant, guinea fowl or a saddle of venison still retain an air of being extra special, so they are ideal for dinner parties. Quail are also an excellent choice as they cook very quickly, taste wonderful and are much meatier than their size would suggest.

ROAST CHICKEN

SERVES 6

1 free-range chicken,
weighing 2.25 kg/5 lb

55 g/2 oz butter

2 tbsp chopped fresh
lemon thyme

1 lemon, quartered

125 ml/4 fl oz white wine

salt and pepper

6 fresh thyme sprigs,
to garnish

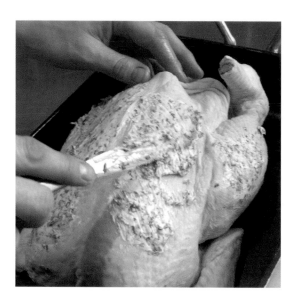

Preheat the oven to 220°C/425°F/Gas Mark 7.
Make sure the chicken is clean, wiping it inside
and out using kitchen paper, and place in a
roasting tin.

Place the butter in a bowl and soften with a
fork, then mix in the thyme and season well with
salt and pepper. Butter the chicken all over with
the herb butter, inside and out, and place the
lemon quarters inside the body cavity. Pour the
wine over the chicken.

Roast the chicken in the centre of the oven
for 20 minutes. Reduce the temperature to
190°C/375°F/Gas Mark 5 and continue to roast
for a further 1 1/4 hours, basting frequently. Cover
with foil if the skin begins to brown too much. If
the tin dries out, add a little more wine or water.

Test that the chicken is cooked by piercing the
thickest part of the leg with a sharp knife or
skewer and making sure the juices run clear.
Remove from the oven.

Remove the chicken from the roasting tin and
place on a warmed serving plate to rest,
covered with foil, for 10 minutes before carving.

Place the roasting tin on the top of the hob
and bubble the pan juices gently over a low heat
until they have reduced and are thick and glossy.
Season to taste with salt and pepper.

Serve the chicken with the pan juices and
scatter with the thyme sprigs.

SIMPLY ROASTED, WITH LOTS OF THYME AND LEMON, CHICKEN PRODUCES A
SUCCULENT GASTRONOMIC FEAST FOR MANY OCCASIONS. TRY TO BUY A GOOD FRESH
CHICKEN AS FROZEN BIRDS DO NOT HAVE AS MUCH FLAVOUR. YOU CAN STUFF YOUR
CHICKEN WITH A TRADITIONAL STUFFING, SUCH AS SAGE AND ONION, OR FRUIT LIKE
APRICOTS AND PRUNES, BUT OFTEN THE BEST WAY IS TO KEEP IT SIMPLE.

POUSSINS WITH HERBS AND WINE

SERVES 4

5 tbsp fresh brown
breadcrumbs

200 g/7 oz low-fat
fromage frais

5 tbsp chopped
fresh parsley

5 tbsp snipped
fresh chives

4 poussins

1 tbsp sunflower oil

675 g/1 lb 8 oz young
spring vegetables, such as
carrots, courgettes, sugar
snap peas, baby sweetcorn
and turnips, cut into
small chunks

125 ml/4 fl oz boiling
chicken stock

2 tsp cornflour

150 ml/5 fl oz dry
white wine

salt and pepper

Preheat the oven to 220°C/425°F/Gas Mark 7.

Mix the breadcrumbs, one-third of the fromage frais and 2 tablespoons each of the parsley and chives together in a bowl. Season well with salt and pepper. Spoon into the neck ends of the poussins. Place on a rack in a roasting tin, brush with the oil and season well with salt and pepper.

Roast in the oven for 30–35 minutes, or until the juices run clear when the thickest part of the meat is pierced with a skewer.

Place the vegetables in a shallow ovenproof dish in a single layer and add half the remaining herbs with the stock.

Cover and bake in the oven for 25–30 minutes until tender. Lift the poussins onto a warmed serving plate and skim any fat from the juices in the tin. Add the vegetable juices and place the tin over a medium heat.

Blend the cornflour with the wine and whisk into the sauce with the remaining fromage frais. Whisk until boiling, then add the remaining herbs. Season to taste with salt and pepper. Spoon the sauce over the poussins and serve with the vegetables.

POUSSINS ARE SIMPLE
TO PREPARE, QUICK TO
COOK AND CAN BE
EASILY CUT IN HALF
LENGTHWAYS WITH A
SHARP KNIFE.

YULETIDE GOOSE WITH HONEY AND PEARS

SERVES 4

1 oven-ready goose, weighing 3.5–4.5 kg/ 7 lb 12 oz–10 lb

1 tsp salt

4 pears

1 tbsp lemon juice

55 g/2 oz butter

2 tbsp clear honey

lemon slices, to garnish

seasonal vegetables, to serve

Preheat the oven to 220°C/425°F/Gas Mark 7.

Rinse the goose and pat dry. Use a fork to prick the skin all over, then rub with the salt. Place the bird upside down on a rack in a roasting tin. Roast in the oven for 30 minutes. Drain off the fat. Turn the bird over and roast for 15 minutes. Drain off the fat. Reduce the temperature to 180°C/350°F/Gas Mark 4 and roast for 15 minutes per 450 g/1 lb. Cover with foil 15 minutes before the end of the cooking time. Check that the bird is cooked by inserting a knife between the legs and body. If the juices run clear, it is cooked. Remove from the oven.

Peel and halve the pears and brush with lemon juice. Melt the butter and honey in a saucepan over a low heat, then add the pears. Cook, stirring, for 5–10 minutes until tender. Remove from the heat, arrange the pears around the goose and pour the sweet juices over the bird. Garnish with lemon slices and serve with seasonal vegetables.

GOOSE FAT IS SIMPLY PERFECT FOR ROASTING (AND SAUTÉING) POTATOES, SO DON'T WASTE IT. POUR ANY THAT YOU ARE NOT ABOUT TO USE IMMEDIATELY INTO A JAR WITH A SCREW TOP AND STORE IN THE REFRIGERATOR.

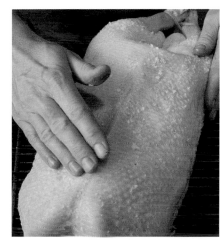

BONED AND STUFFED ROAST DUCKLING

SERVES 6–8

1 duckling, weighing 1.8 kg/4 lb (dressed weight); ask your butcher to bone the duckling and cut off the wings at the first joint

450 g/1 lb flavoured sausage meat

1 small onion, finely chopped

1 Cox's apple, cored and finely chopped

85 g/3 oz ready-to-eat dried apricots, finely chopped

85 g/3 oz chopped walnuts

2 tbsp chopped fresh parsley

1 large or 2 smaller duck breasts, skin removed

salt and pepper

Apricot sauce

400 g/14 oz canned apricot halves

150 ml/5 fl oz stock

125 ml/4 fl oz Marsala

1/2 tsp ground cinammon

1/2 tsp ground ginger

salt and pepper

Wipe the duckling with kitchen paper both inside and out. Lay it skin-side down on a board and season well with salt and pepper.

Mix the sausage meat, onion, apple, apricots, walnuts and parsley together. Season well with salt and pepper. Form into a large sausage shape.

Lay the duck breast(s) on the whole duckling and cover with the stuffing. Wrap the whole duckling around the stuffing and carefully tuck in any leg and neck flaps.

Preheat the oven to 190°C/375°F/Gas Mark 5.

Sew the duckling up the back and across both ends with fine string. Try to use one piece of string so that you can remove it in one go. Mould the duckling into a good shape and place, sewn-side down, on a wire rack over a roasting tin.

Roast in the oven for 1 1/2–2 hours, basting occasionally. Pour off some of the fat in the tin. When it is cooked, the duckling should be golden brown and the skin crisp.

Purée the apricots with syrup in a blender or food processor. Pour into a saucepan, add the stock, Marsala, cinnamon and ginger and season with salt and pepper. Stir over a low heat, then simmer for 2–3 minutes.

Carve the duckling into thick slices at the table and serve with warm Apricot Sauce.

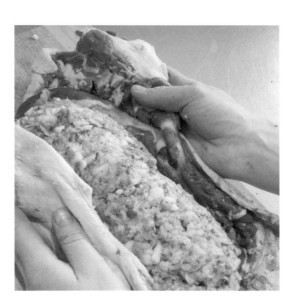

DUCKLING IS WONDERFUL TO SERVE ON A SPECIAL OCCASION, THE ONLY DRAWBACK BEING THAT THERE IS NOT MUCH MEAT ON THE BIRD AND IT CAN BE DIFFICULT TO CARVE. WHY NOT HAVE YOUR BUTCHER BONE THE DUCKLING FOR YOU AND THEN STUFF IT WITH GOOD-QUALITY SAUSAGE MEAT? IF YOU ADD A COUPLE OF DUCK BREASTS, YOU CAN MAKE A VERY SUBSTANTIAL DISH FOR 6–8 PEOPLE THAT IS EASY TO CARVE AND LOOKS WONDERFUL. SERVE WITH A SWEET SAUCE – ORANGE IS CLASSIC, BUT ONE MADE WITH CANNED APRICOTS, SPICED WITH CINNAMON AND GINGER, IS MORE UNUSUAL.

TRADITIONAL ROAST TURKEY
WITH WINE AND MUSHROOMS

SERVES 4

1 oven-ready turkey,
weighing 5 kg/11 lb

1 garlic clove,
finely chopped

100 ml/3¹/₂ fl oz red wine

75 g/2¹/₂ oz butter

Stuffing

100 g/3¹/₂ oz button
mushrooms

1 onion, chopped

1 garlic clove, chopped

85 g/3 oz butter

100 g/3¹/₂ oz fresh
breadcrumbs

2 tbsp finely chopped
fresh sage

1 tbsp lemon juice

salt and pepper

Port and cranberry sauce

100 g/3¹/₂ oz sugar

250 ml/9 fl oz port

175 g/6 oz fresh
cranberries

Preheat the oven to 200°C/400°F/Gas Mark 6.

To make the stuffing, clean and chop the mushrooms, put them in a saucepan with the onion, garlic and butter and cook for 3 minutes.

Remove from the heat and stir in the remaining stuffing ingredients. Rinse the turkey and pat dry with kitchen paper. Fill the neck end with stuffing and truss with string.

Put the turkey in a roasting tin. Rub the garlic over the bird and pour the wine over. Add the butter and roast in the oven for 30 minutes. Baste, then reduce the temperature to 180°C/350°F/Gas Mark 4 and roast for a further 40 minutes. Baste again and cover with foil. Roast for a further 2 hours, basting regularly. Check that the bird is cooked by inserting a knife between the legs and body. If the juices run clear, it is cooked. Remove from the oven, cover with foil and leave to stand for 25 minutes.

Meanwhile, put the sugar, port and cranberries in a saucepan. Heat over a medium heat until almost boiling. Reduce the heat, simmer for 15 minutes, stirring, then remove from the heat. Serve with the turkey.

THE MAJORITY OF TURKEYS ON SALE ARE WHITE-FEATHERED VARIETIES. HOWEVER, THE DARK-FEATHERED BIRDS, KNOWN AS BRONZE TURKEYS, ARE BECOMING INCREASINGLY POPULAR. THE SKIN MAY SHOW THE REMAINS OF DARK STUBBLE, WHICH LOOKS LESS ATTRACTIVE, BUT THE FLAVOUR OF BRONZE BIRDS IS USUALLY SUPERIOR. NORFOLK BRONZE AND NORFOLK BLACK ARE BOTH FLAVOURSOME, PLUMP-BREASTED BREEDS.

ROAST TURKEY
WITH CIDER SAUCE

SERVES 8

1 boneless turkey breast
roast, weighing 1 kg/
2 lb 4 oz

1 tbsp sunflower or
corn oil

salt and pepper

Stuffing

25 g/1 oz butter

2 shallots, finely chopped

1 celery stick,
finely chopped

1 cooking apple, peeled,
cored and diced

115 g/4 oz prunes, stoned
and chopped

55 g/2 oz raisins

3 tbsp chicken stock

4 tbsp dry cider

1 tbsp chopped
fresh parsley

Cider sauce

1 shallot, very finely
chopped

300 ml/10 fl oz dry cider

125 ml/4 fl oz chicken
stock

1 tsp cider vinegar

Preheat the oven to 190°C/375°F/Gas Mark 5.

To make the stuffing, melt the butter in a saucepan. Add the shallots and cook, stirring occasionally, for 5 minutes. Add the celery and apple and cook for 5 minutes. Add the remaining stuffing ingredients, cover and simmer gently for 5 minutes, or until all the liquid has been absorbed. Transfer to a bowl and leave to cool.

Place the turkey roast on a chopping board and slice almost completely through, from the thin side towards the thicker side. Open out, place between 2 sheets of clingfilm and flatten with a meat mallet or rolling pin to an even thickness. Season to taste with salt. Spoon on

the cooled stuffing, roll the roast around it and tie with kitchen string. Heat the oil in a roasting tin over a medium heat, add the roast and brown all over. Transfer to the oven and roast for 1 hour 10 minutes, or until cooked through and the juices run clear when the meat is pierced with a skewer.

Remove the roast from the tin and cover with foil. To make the sauce, pour off any fat from the tin and set over a medium heat. Add the shallot and half the cider and cook for 1–2 minutes, scraping any sediment from the base of the tin. Add the remaining cider, stock and vinegar and cook for 10 minutes, or until reduced and thickened. Remove and discard the string from the turkey and cut into slices. Serve with the cider sauce.

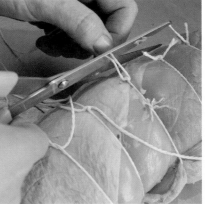

MOST SUPERMARKETS SELL BONELESS TURKEY BREAST ROAST. THERE IS NO WASTE, SO IT IS AN ECONOMICAL CHOICE WHEN ENTERTAINING AND IT FITS INTO THE OVEN MORE EASILY THAN A WHOLE BIRD. ROLLING THE TURKEY AROUND THE STUFFING HELPS TO KEEP THE MEAT MOIST DURING COOKING.

ROAST PHEASANT
WITH RED WINE AND HERBS

SERVES 4

100 g/3½ oz butter,
slightly softened

1 tbsp chopped
fresh thyme

1 tbsp chopped
fresh parsley

2 oven-ready young
pheasants

4 tbsp vegetable oil

125 ml/4 fl oz red wine

salt and pepper

To serve

honey-glazed parsnips

sautéed potatoes

freshly cooked
Brussels sprouts

Preheat the oven to 190°C/375°F/Gas Mark 5.

Put the butter in a small bowl and mix in the chopped herbs. Lift the skins off the pheasants, taking care not to tear them, and push the herb butter under the skins. Season to taste with salt and pepper. Pour the oil into a roasting tin, add the pheasants and cook in the oven for 45 minutes, basting occasionally.

Remove from the oven, pour over the wine, then return to the oven and cook for a further 15 minutes, or until cooked through. Check that each bird is cooked by inserting a knife between the legs and body. If the juices run clear, they are cooked.

Remove the pheasants from the oven, cover with foil and leave to stand for 15 minutes. Divide between individual serving plates, and serve with honey-glazed parsnips, sautéed potatoes and freshly cooked Brussels sprouts.

ONLY YOUNG BIRDS ARE SUITABLE FOR ROASTING, AS OLDER PHEASANTS ARE FAIRLY TOUGH AND NEED A SLOWER COOKING METHOD. EVEN SO, THE MEAT ON THE LEGS TENDS TO BE QUITE TOUGH AND SINEWY, WHEREAS THE LIGHTER BREASTS ARE MORE DELICATE AND TENDER. IT IS QUITE USUAL TO SERVE ONLY THE BREASTS. KEEP THE LEG MEAT FOR MAKING A MINCED PASTA SAUCE OR USING IN A PIE. YOU CAN ALSO MAKE DELICIOUS STOCK WITH THE CARCASSES.

GUINEA FOWL WITH CABBAGE

SERVES 4

1 oven-ready guinea fowl, weighing 1.25 kg/2 lb 12 oz

¹/₂ tbsp sunflower oil

¹/₂ apple, peeled, cored and chopped

several fresh flat-leaf parsley sprigs, stems bruised

1 large Savoy cabbage, coarse outer leaves removed, cored and quartered

1 thick piece of smoked belly of pork, weighing about 140 g/5 oz, rind removed and cut into thin lardons, or 140 g/5 oz unsmoked lardons

1 onion, sliced

1 bouquet garni

1¹/₂ tbsp chopped fresh flat-leaf parsley

salt and pepper

Preheat the oven to 240°C/475°F/Gas Mark 9.

Rub the guinea fowl with the oil and season to taste inside and out with salt and pepper. Add the apple and parsley sprigs to the guinea fowl's cavity and truss to tie the legs together. Place the guinea fowl in a roasting tin and roast in the oven for 20 minutes to colour the breasts. When the guinea fowl is golden brown, reduce the oven temperature to 160°C/325°F/Gas Mark 3.

Meanwhile, bring a large saucepan of salted water to the boil. Add the cabbage and blanch for 3 minutes. Drain, rinse in cold water and pat dry.

Place the lardons in a flameproof casserole over a medium-high heat and sauté until they give off their fat. Use a slotted spoon to remove the lardons from the casserole and set aside.

Add the onion to the fat left in the casserole and cook, stirring frequently, for 5 minutes, or until the onion is tender, but not brown. Stir the bouquet garni into the casserole with a very little salt and a pinch of pepper, then return the lardons to the casserole.

Remove the guinea fowl from the oven. Add the cabbage to the casserole, top with the guinea fowl and cover the surface with a piece of wet greaseproof paper. Cover the casserole and put it in the oven for 45 minutes–1 hour, or until the guinea fowl is tender and the juices run clear when a skewer is inserted into the thickest part of the meat.

Remove the guinea fowl from the casserole and cut into serving portions. Stir the parsley into the cabbage and onion, then taste and adjust the seasoning if necessary. Serve the guinea fowl portions on a bed of cabbage and onion.

IT IS IMPORTANT NOT TO ADD TOO MUCH SALT TO THE ONION AS THE LARDONS WILL BE SALTY.

QUAIL WITH GRAPES

SERVES 4

4 tbsp olive oil

8 oven-ready quail

280 g/10 oz green seedless grapes

225 ml/8 fl oz grape juice

2 cloves

about 150 ml/5 fl oz water

2 tbsp brandy

salt and pepper

Potato pancake

600 g/1 lb 5 oz unpeeled potatoes

35 g/1¼ oz unsalted butter or pork fat

1¼ tbsp olive oil

Preheat the oven to 230°C/450°F/Gas Mark 8. Parboil the potatoes for the pancake in a large saucepan of lightly salted water for 10 minutes. Drain and leave to cool completely, then peel, coarsely grate and season to taste with salt and pepper. Set aside.

Heat the oil in a heavy-based frying pan or flameproof casserole large enough to hold the quail in a single layer over a medium heat. Add the quail and fry on all sides until golden brown.

Add the grapes, grape juice, cloves, enough water to come halfway up the sides of the quail and salt and pepper to taste. Cover and simmer for 20 minutes. Transfer the quail and all the juices to a roasting tin and sprinkle with the brandy. Place in the oven and roast, uncovered, for 10 minutes.

Meanwhile, to make the potato pancake, melt the butter with the oil in a 30-cm/12-inch non-stick frying pan over a high heat. When the fat is hot, add the potatoes and spread into an even layer. Reduce the heat and cook gently for 10 minutes. Place a plate over the frying pan and, wearing oven gloves, invert them so that the potato pancake drops onto the plate. Slide the potato back into the frying pan and continue cooking for 10 minutes, or until cooked through and crisp. Slide out of the frying pan and cut into 4 wedges. Keep warm until the quail are ready.

Place a potato pancake wedge and 2 quail on each plate. Taste the grape sauce and adjust the seasoning if necessary. Spoon the sauce over the quail and serve.

FARMED QUAIL, WEIGHING 115–140 G/4–5 OZ, ARE WIDELY AVAILABLE ALL YEAR ROUND. THEY MAY BE FRESH OR FROZEN AND ARE USUALLY OVEN-READY.

ROAST VENISON WITH BRANDY SAUCE

SERVES 4

6 tbsp vegetable oil

1.7 kg/3 lb 12 oz saddle
of fresh venison, trimmed

salt and pepper

fresh thyme sprigs,
to garnish

freshly cooked vegetables,
to serve

Brandy sauce

4 tbsp vegetable stock

1 tbsp plain flour

175 ml/6 fl oz brandy

100 ml/3¹/₂ fl oz double
cream

Preheat the oven to 180°C/350°F/Gas Mark 4.
Heat half the oil in a frying pan over a high heat. Season the venison to taste with salt and pepper, add to the pan and cook until lightly browned all over. Pour the remaining oil into a roasting pan. Add the venison, cover with foil and roast in the oven, basting occasionally, for 1¹/₂ hours, or until cooked through. Remove

from the oven and transfer to a warmed serving platter. Cover with foil and set aside.

To make the sauce, stir the flour into the roasting pan over the hob and cook for 1 minute. Pour in the stock and heat it, stirring to loosen the sediment from the base. Gradually stir in the brandy and bring to the boil, then reduce the heat and simmer, stirring, for 10–15 minutes until the sauce has thickened a little. Remove from the heat and stir in the cream.

Garnish the venison with thyme and serve with the brandy sauce and a selection of freshly cooked vegetables.

BOTH WILD AND FARMED VENISON – DEER MEAT – ARE AVAILABLE AND SURPRISINGLY INEXPENSIVE COMPARED WITH LAMB OR BEEF. IT MAY BE FRESH OR FROZEN. IT HAS A DELICATE TEXTURE AND IS HIGH IN PROTEIN, BUT LOW IN FAT, SO IT IS VERY NUTRITIOUS.

We tend to think of roasting fish as a fairly modern technique, yet even Mrs Beeton in her famous 19th-century enquire-within on household management includes recipes for roasting salmon, sole and mackerel, although she tends to call the process baking. This signposts the differences between roasting meat or poultry and roasting fish. Firstly, fish cooks very much more rapidly than most meat and, secondly, its flesh is generally quite delicate and can easily be dried out by the high heat of the oven. Therefore, many recipes include extra ingredients, such as lemon or lime juice, wine, vegetables, breadcrumbs and herbs, as well as oil or butter, to protect it and keep it moist. These may be used as stuffings, crusts or sauces, or as a mixture of these.

You need to pay attention to the roasting times and to keep an eye on the fish while it is cooking, but roasting fish is not a difficult art and

PART THREE
THE OCEAN SELECTION

the results are simply mouthwatering. The crisp golden skin enclosing the succulent flesh of a well-roasted whole fish makes sea bass or sea bream a spectacular dinner party dish, while fillets of all kinds, whether oily or white fish, are easy to handle and serve. In particular, meaty fish with firm flesh respond well to roasting – monkfish perhaps being the best of all, although tuna runs a close second. The texture of monkfish and even its flavour have been compared – favourably – to that of roast lamb. Seafood, such as prawns, acquires a special flavour when roasted, with the added advantage that it takes hardly any time to cook, and there is no need to stand over it and stir.

ROASTED SEA BASS

SERVES 4

1 whole sea bass, about
1.3–1.8 kg/3–4 lb, cleaned

1 small onion,
finely chopped

2 garlic cloves,
finely chopped

2 tbsp finely chopped
fresh herbs, such
as parsley, chervil
and tarragon

25 g/1 oz anchovy fillets,
finely chopped

25 g/1 oz butter

150 ml/5 fl oz white wine

2 tbsp crème fraîche

salt and pepper

Preheat the oven to 200°C/400°F/Gas Mark 6.

Remove any scales from the fish and rinse it thoroughly both inside and out. If you like, trim off the fins with a pair of scissors. Using a sharp knife, make five or six cuts diagonally into the flesh of the fish on both sides. Season well with salt and pepper, both inside and out.

Mix the onion, garlic, herbs and anchovies together in a bowl.

Stuff the fish with half the mixture and spoon the remainder into a roasting tin. Place the sea bass on top.

Spread the butter over the fish, pour over the wine and place in the oven. Roast for 30–35 minutes until the fish is cooked through and the flesh flakes easily.

Using a fish slice, carefully remove the sea bass from the tin to a warmed serving platter. Place the roasting tin over a medium heat and stir the onion mixture and juices together. Add the crème fraîche, mix well and pour into a warmed serving bowl.

Serve the sea bass whole and divide at the table. Spoon a little sauce on the side.

YOU CAN USE EITHER SMALL INDIVIDUAL FISH TO SERVE AS SINGLE PORTIONS OR ONE LARGE ONE TO SHARE AMONG FAMILY OR FRIENDS. INDIVIDUAL FISH, WEIGHING 280–350 G/10–12 OZ EACH, WILL TAKE ONLY 15–20 MINUTES TO ROAST. ROUND FISH LIKE SEA BASS, SEA BREAM, RED MULLET, RED SNAPPER, TROUT AND MACKEREL ARE PARTICULARLY GOOD FOR ROASTING AS THEIR SKIN CRISPS UP WELL WHILE THE FLESH STAYS DELICIOUSLY MOIST AND CREAMY. MAKE SURE YOU USE REALLY FRESH FISH IF YOU WANT THIS DISH TO SPARKLE.

ROASTED SALMON WITH LEMON AND HERBS

SERVES 4

6 tbsp extra virgin
olive oil

1 onion, sliced

1 leek, sliced

juice of 1/2 lemon

2 tbsp chopped
fresh parsley

2 tbsp chopped fresh dill

500 g/1 lb 2 oz salmon
fillets

salt and pepper

freshly cooked baby
spinach leaves, to serve

To garnish

lemon slices

fresh dill sprigs

Preheat the oven to 200°C/400°F/Gas Mark 6.

Heat 1 tablespoon of the oil in a frying pan over a medium heat. Add the onion and leek and cook, stirring occasionally, for 4 minutes, or until slightly softened.

Meanwhile, put the remaining oil in a small bowl with the lemon juice and herbs and season to taste with salt and pepper. Stir together well. Rinse the fish under cold running water, then pat dry with kitchen paper. Arrange the fish in a shallow ovenproof dish.

Remove the frying pan from the heat and spread the onion and leek over the fish. Pour the oil mixture over the top, making sure that everything is well coated. Roast in the centre of the preheated oven for 10 minutes, or until the fish is cooked through.

Arrange the cooked spinach on serving plates. Remove the fish and vegetables from the oven and arrange on top of the spinach. Garnish with lemon slices and sprigs of dill. Serve immediately.

ALTHOUGH SALMON IS AN OILY FISH, IT HAS VERY DELICATE FLESH THAT CAN DRY OUT EASILY. THEREFORE, IT IS IMPORTANT TO MAKE SURE THAT ALL THE FILLETS ARE WELL COATED WITH THE OIL AND LEMON JUICE MIXTURE TO PROTECT THEM. KEEP AN EYE ON THE FISH DURING ROASTING TO PREVENT OVERCOOKING.

ROASTED TUNA WITH ORANGE AND ANCHOVIES

SERVES 4–6

200 ml/7 fl oz freshly squeezed orange juice

3 tbsp extra virgin olive oil

55 g/2 oz anchovy fillets in oil, roughly chopped, with the oil reserved

small pinch of dried chilli flakes, or to taste

1 tuna fillet, about 600 g/1 lb 5 oz

pepper

Combine the orange juice, 2 tablespoons of the olive oil, the anchovies and their oil and chilli flakes in a non-metallic bowl large enough to hold the tuna and add pepper to taste. Add the tuna and spoon the marinade over it. Cover with clingfilm and chill in the refrigerator for at least 2 hours to marinate, turning the tuna occasionally. Remove the bowl from the refrigerator about 20 minutes before cooking to return the fish to room temperature.

Meanwhile, preheat the oven to 220°C/425°F/Gas Mark 7.

Remove the tuna from the marinade, reserving the marinade, and wipe dry. Heat the remaining oil in a large frying pan over a high heat. Add the tuna and sear for 1 minute on each side until lightly browned and crisp. Place in a small roasting tin. Cover the tin tightly with foil.

Roast in the oven for 8 minutes for medium-rare and 10 minutes for medium-well done. Remove from the oven and set aside to rest for at least 2 minutes before slicing.

Meanwhile, put the marinade in a small saucepan over a high heat and bring to a rolling boil. Boil for at least 2 minutes.

Transfer the tuna to a serving platter and carve into thick slices, which will probably break into chunks as you cut them. Serve the sauce separately for spooning over. The tuna can be served hot or at room temperature, but the sauce is best hot.

JUST LIKE BEEF, ROASTED TUNA CONTINUES TO COOK AFTER IT COMES OUT OF THE OVEN WHILE IT RESTS. AN EASY WAY TO CHECK WHETHER THE TUNA IS COOKED IS TO INSERT A MEAT THERMOMETER INTO IT, THROUGH THE FOIL, JUST BEFORE YOU PUT THE COVERED TIN IN THE OVEN. WHEN THE TEMPERATURE READS 60°C/140°F, THE TUNA WILL BE MEDIUM.

ROASTED SEAFOOD

SERVES 4

600 g/1 lb 5 oz new potatoes

3 red onions, cut into wedges

2 courgettes, cut into chunks

8 garlic cloves, peeled but left whole

2 lemons, cut into wedges

4 fresh rosemary sprigs

4 tbsp olive oil

350 g/12 oz unpeeled raw prawns

2 small raw squid, cut into rings

4 tomatoes, quartered

Preheat the oven to 200°C/400°F/Gas Mark 6.
Scrub the potatoes to remove any dirt. Cut any large potatoes in half. Parboil the potatoes in a saucepan of boiling water for 10–15 minutes. Place the potatoes in a large roasting

tin together with the onions, courgettes, garlic, lemons and rosemary sprigs.

Pour over the oil and toss to coat all the vegetables in it. Roast in the oven for 30 minutes, turning occasionally, until the potatoes are tender.

Once the potatoes are tender, add the prawns, squid and tomatoes, tossing to coat them in the oil, and roast for 10 minutes. All the vegetables should be cooked through and slightly charred for full flavour.

Transfer the roasted seafood and vegetables to warmed serving plates and serve hot.

MOST VEGETABLES ARE SUITABLE FOR ROASTING IN THE OVEN. TRY ADDING 450 G/1 LB PUMPKIN, SQUASH OR AUBERGINE, IF YOU LIKE.

ROAST MONKFISH
WITH ROMESCO SAUCE

SERVES 4–6

1 monkfish tail, about 900 g/2 lb, membrane removed

2–3 slices serrano ham

olive oil, for brushing

salt and pepper

Romesco sauce

1 red pepper, halved and deseeded

4 garlic cloves, unpeeled

2 tomatoes, halved

125 ml/4 fl oz olive oil

1 slice white bread, diced

4 tbsp blanched almonds

1 fresh red chilli, deseeded and chopped

2 shallots, chopped

1 tsp paprika

2 tbsp red wine vinegar

2 tsp sugar

1 tbsp water

Preheat the oven to 220°C/ 425°F/Gas Mark 7.

For the sauce, put the pepper, garlic and tomatoes in a roasting tin and toss with 1 tablespoon of the oil. Roast in the oven for 20–25 minutes, then remove from the oven, cover with a tea towel and set aside for 10 minutes. Peel off the skins and place the vegetables in a food processor.

Heat 1 tablespoon of the remaining oil in a frying pan. Add the bread cubes and almonds and cook over a low heat, stirring frequently, until golden. Remove with a slotted spoon and drain on kitchen paper. Add the chilli, shallots and paprika to the frying pan and cook, stirring occasionally, for 5 minutes.

Transfer the bread and chilli mixtures to the food processor, add the vinegar, sugar and water and process to a paste. With the motor running, add the remaining oil through the feeder tube. Set aside.

Reduce the oven temperature to 200°C/ 400°F/Gas Mark 6. Rinse the monkfish tail and pat it dry. Wrap the ham around the monkfish and brush lightly with oil. Season to taste with salt and pepper. Put the fish on a baking sheet.

Roast the monkfish in the oven for 20 minutes until the flesh is opaque and flakes easily. Test by lifting off the ham along the central bone and cut a small amount of the flesh away from the bone to see if it flakes.

Cut through the ham to remove the central bone and produce 2 thick fillets. Cut each fillet into 2 or 3 pieces and arrange on plates with a spoonful of Romesco Sauce. Serve immediately.

SERVE THIS WITH CHILLI ROAST POTATOES (SEE PAGE 80) OR BOILED LONG-GRAIN RICE WITH CHOPPED FRESH HERBS ADDED.

GARLIC-CRUSTED
ROAST HADDOCK

SERVES 4

900 g/2 lb floury potatoes

125 ml/4 fl oz milk

55 g/2 oz butter

4 haddock fillets, about
225 g/8 oz each

1 tbsp sunflower oil

4 garlic cloves,
finely chopped

salt and pepper

2 tbsp chopped fresh
parsley, to garnish

Preheat the oven to 230°C/450°F/Gas Mark 8.

Cut the potatoes into chunks and cook in a saucepan of lightly salted water for 15 minutes, or until tender. Drain well. Mash in the saucepan until smooth. Set over a low heat and beat in the milk, butter and salt and pepper to taste.

Put the haddock fillets in a roasting tin and brush the fish with the oil. Sprinkle the garlic on top, add salt and pepper to taste, then spread with the mashed potatoes. Roast in the oven for 8–10 minutes, or until the fish is just tender.

Meanwhile, preheat the grill. Transfer the fish to the grill and cook for about 2 minutes, or until golden brown. Sprinkle with the chopped parsley and serve immediately.

IF YOU PREFER, YOU CAN COOK THE POTATOES UNPEELED, BUT DO SCRUB THEM FIRST. PEEL THEM AS SOON AS THEY ARE COOL ENOUGH TO HANDLE, THEN MASH AS ABOVE. THIS HELPS TO PRESERVE THE VITAMINS AND MINERALS THAT LIE JUST BENEATH THE SKIN.

ROAST SEA BREAM
WITH FENNEL

SERVES 4

250 g/9 oz dry,
uncoloured breadcrumbs

2 tbsp milk

1 fennel bulb, thinly
sliced, fronds reserved
for garnishing

1 tbsp lemon juice

2 tbsp sambuca

1 tbsp chopped
fresh thyme

1 dried bay leaf, crumbled

1 whole sea bream, about
1.5 kg/3 lb 5 oz, cleaned,
scaled and boned

3 tbsp olive oil, plus extra
for brushing

1 red onion, chopped

300 ml/10 fl oz dry
white wine

salt and pepper

lemon wedges, to serve

Preheat the oven to 240°C/475°F/Gas Mark 9.

Place the breadcrumbs in a bowl, add the milk and set aside for 5 minutes to soak. Place the fennel in another bowl and add the lemon juice, sambuca, thyme and bay leaf. Squeeze the breadcrumbs and add them to the fennel mixture, stirring well.

Rinse the fish inside and out under cold running water and pat dry with kitchen paper. Season to taste with salt and pepper. Spoon the fennel mixture into the cavity, then bind the fish with trussing thread or kitchen string.

Brush a large ovenproof dish with oil and sprinkle the onion over the base. Lay the fish on top and pour in the wine – it should reach about one-third of the way up the fish. Drizzle the fish with the oil and roast in the oven for 25–30 minutes. Baste the fish occasionally with the cooking juices, and if it begins to brown, cover with a piece of foil to protect it.

Carefully lift out the sea bream with a fish slice, remove the string and place on a warmed serving platter. Garnish with the reserved fennel fronds and serve immediately with lemon wedges for squeezing over the fish.

SAMBUCA IS AN ITALIAN LIQUEUR DISTILLED FROM WITCH ELDER, BUT IT HAS A STRONG ANISEED FLAVOUR, WHICH MARRIES WELL WITH FISH. IF IT IS UNAVAILABLE, SUBSTITUTE PERNOD.

ITALIAN COD

SERVES 4

25 g/1 oz butter

50 g/1³/4 oz fresh
wholemeal breadcrumbs

25 g/1 oz chopped
walnuts

grated rind and juice of
2 lemons

2 fresh rosemary sprigs,
stalks removed

2 tbsp chopped
fresh parsley

4 cod fillets, about 150 g/
5¹/2 oz each

1 garlic clove, crushed

1 small fresh red chilli,
diced

3 tbsp walnut oil

mixed salad leaves,
to serve

Preheat the oven to 200°C/400°F/Gas Mark 6.

Melt the butter in a large saucepan over a low heat, stirring constantly. Remove the pan from the heat and add the breadcrumbs, walnuts, the rind and juice of 1 lemon, half the rosemary and half the parsley, stirring to mix.

Press the breadcrumb mixture over the top of the cod fillets. Place the cod fillets in a shallow foil-lined roasting tin.

Roast the fish in the oven for 25–30 minutes.

Mix the garlic, the remaining lemon rind and juice, rosemary, parsley and the chilli together in a bowl. Beat in the oil and mix to combine. Drizzle the dressing over the cod steaks as soon as they are cooked.

Transfer the fish to warmed serving plates and serve immediately with salad leaves.

IF PREFERRED, THE WALNUTS
MAY BE OMITTED FROM THE
CRUST. IN ADDITION, EXTRA
VIRGIN OLIVE OIL CAN BE
USED INSTEAD OF WALNUT
OIL, IF YOU LIKE.

ROASTED MACKEREL MEDITERRANEAN-STYLE

SERVES 4

4 tbsp basil oil or extra virgin olive oil

2 garlic cloves, chopped

1 onion, sliced

2 courgettes, sliced

6 plum tomatoes, sliced

12 black olives, stoned and halved

1 tbsp tomato purée

4 tbsp red wine

100 ml/3 1/2 fl oz fish stock

2 tbsp chopped fresh parsley

2 tbsp chopped fresh basil

4 large mackerel, cleaned

salt and pepper

To garnish

lemon slices

fresh basil sprigs

To serve

freshly cooked spaghetti

salad leaves and spring onions

Preheat the oven to 200°C/400°F/Gas Mark 6.

Heat 1 tablespoon of the oil in a large frying pan over a medium heat. Add the garlic, onion and courgettes and cook, stirring occasionally, for 4 minutes. Add the tomatoes, olives, tomato purée, wine, stock, herbs and salt and pepper to taste. Bring to the boil, then reduce the heat to medium. Cook, stirring frequently, for 10 minutes.

Rinse the fish under cold running water, then pat dry with kitchen paper. Arrange the fish in a shallow ovenproof dish and drizzle the remaining oil over. Remove the frying pan from the heat and spread the tomato sauce over the fish. Roast the fish in the centre of the preheated oven for 10 minutes, or until they are cooked through.

Remove from the oven, arrange the fish in their sauce on plates of freshly cooked spaghetti and garnish with lemon slices and sprigs of basil. Serve accompanied by a side salad of salad leaves and spring onions.

THE MEDITERRANEAN DIET IS SAID TO BE AMONG THE HEALTHIEST – THIS DISH IS A PERFECT EXAMPLE. MACKEREL PROVIDES ESSENTIAL FATTY ACIDS, OLIVE OIL IS HIGH IN VITAMIN A AND MONOUNSATURATED ('GOOD') FATS, WHILE TOMATOES, ESPECIALLY COOKED ONES, HAVE MANY HEALTH-ENHANCING PROPERTIES.

FISH ROASTED WITH LIME

SERVES 4

1 kg/2 lb 4 oz white fish
fillets, such as bass, plaice
or cod

1 lime, halved

3 tbsp extra virgin
olive oil

1 large onion,
finely chopped

3 garlic cloves,
finely chopped

2–3 pickled jalapeño
chillies (jalapeños en
escabeche), chopped

6–8 tbsp chopped
fresh coriander

salt and pepper

lemon and lime wedges,
to serve

Preheat the oven to 180°C/350°F/Gas Mark 4.

Place the fish fillets in a non-metallic bowl and season to taste with salt and pepper. Squeeze the juice from the lime halves over the fish.

Heat the oil in a frying pan. Add the onion and garlic and cook, stirring frequently, for

2 minutes, or until softened. Remove the frying pan from the heat.

Place a third of the onion mixture and a little of the chillies and coriander in the base of a shallow ovenproof dish or roasting tin. Arrange the fish on top. Top with the remaining onion mixture, chillies and coriander.

Roast in the oven for 15–20 minutes, or until the fish has become slightly opaque and firm to the touch. Serve immediately, with lemon and lime wedges for squeezing over the fish.

TANGY AND SIMPLE TO PREPARE, THIS IS EXCELLENT SERVED WITH RICE AND BEANS FOR AN EASY LUNCH – SERVE WITH A GLASS OF CHILLED BEER.

No book about roasting food would be complete without roast potatoes, the perfect partner for roast meat and poultry. The many fans of this vegetable will be delighted to discover that there is more than one way to enjoy this superb accompaniment to a wide variety of dishes. Roast potatoes, served hot or cold, also make the most delicious snacks when sprinkled with salt and eaten with the fingers.

Other vegetables also lend themselves to this method of cooking. Roasting brings out the full flavour and a delightful sweetness in many root vegetables, such as carrots, parsnips, turnips and sweet potatoes. Squashes, from butternuts to courgettes, and Mediterranean vegetables, such as tomatoes, aubergines and peppers, make wonderful medleys that can be served as a vegetarian main course or as a side dish.

Still other vegetables, from onions to fennel, work well on their own. Roasting not only

PART FOUR
FRESH FROM THE GARDEN

develops a succulent depth of flavour, but often also creates an unusual crisp texture.

Serving roast vegetables, as a colourful mix or as individual high notes, with roast meat, poultry, game or fish makes economic sense, too. If the oven will be switched on anyway, why not make full use of the space available? This helps save the housekeeping budget and uses fewer fuel resources. It also makes preparing a meal for family or guests almost trouble free, as roasting rarely requires a lot of attention and time in the kitchen. Mix and match the recipes from earlier chapters with those in this one, keeping an eye open for compatible oven temperatures and checking cooking times.

PERFECT ROAST POTATOES

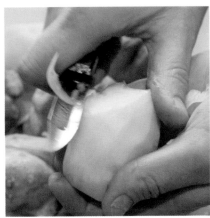

Drain the potatoes well and return them to the saucepan. Cover with the lid and firmly shake the pan so that the surface of the potatoes is slightly roughened to help give a much crisper texture.

Remove the roasting tin from the oven and carefully tip the potatoes into the hot fat. Baste them to ensure that they are all coated with it.

Roast the potatoes at the top of the oven for 45–50 minutes until they are browned all over and thoroughly crisp. Turn the potatoes and baste again only once during the process or the crunchy edges will be destroyed.

Using a slotted spoon, carefully transfer the potatoes from the roasting tin into a warmed serving dish. Sprinkle with a little salt and serve immediately. Any leftovers (although this is most unlikely) are delicious cold.

SERVES 6

1.3 kg/3 lb large floury potatoes, such as King Edwards, Maris Piper or Desirée, peeled and cut into even-sized chunks

3 tbsp dripping, goose fat, duck fat or olive oil

salt

Preheat the oven to 220°C/425°F/Gas Mark 7.

Cook the potatoes in a large saucepan of lightly salted boiling water over a medium heat, covered, for 5–7 minutes. They will still be firm. Remove from the heat. Meanwhile, add the fat to a roasting tin and place in the hot oven.

PERFECT ROAST POTATOES ARE CRISP ON THE OUTSIDE AND SOFT AND FLUFFY ON THE INSIDE. DO CHOOSE THE RIGHT POTATOES – FLOURY ONES ARE BEST. THE CHOICE OF FAT IS ALSO IMPORTANT – GOOSE OR DUCK FAT GIVES AN AMAZING FLAVOUR. HOWEVER, THE FAT FROM A JOINT IS ALMOST AS GOOD AND REALLY TASTY POTATOES CAN ALSO BE MADE USING OLIVE OIL. PARBOILING THE POTATOES IS A CHORE BUT WORTHWHILE BECAUSE IT GIVES CRUSTY OUTSIDES. HOWEVER, IF YOU REALLY CAN'T BEAR TO DO IT, SUBSTITUTE SMALL, WHOLE, UNPEELED NEW POTATOES, WHICH DO NOT NEED PARBOILING. SIMPLY COAT THEM IN THE HOT FAT AND ROAST FOR 30–40 MINUTES. IN BOTH CASES, A HEAVY ROASTING TIN WILL ENSURE THAT THE POTATOES DON'T STICK, AND A HOT OVEN MEANS THAT THEY CRISP, NOT STEAM, IN THE FAT.

ROASTED GARLIC MASHED POTATOES

SERVES 4

2 whole garlic bulbs

1 tbsp olive oil

900 g/2 lb floury potatoes, peeled

125 ml/4 fl oz milk

55 g/2 oz butter

salt and pepper

Preheat the oven to 180°C/350°F/Gas Mark 4.

Separate the garlic cloves, place on a large piece of foil and drizzle with the oil. Wrap the garlic in the foil and roast in the oven for about 1 hour, or until very tender. Leave to cool slightly.

Twenty minutes before the end of the cooking time, cut the potatoes into chunks, then cook in a saucepan of lightly salted boiling water for 15 minutes, or until tender.

Meanwhile, squeeze the cooled garlic cloves out of their skins and push through a sieve into a saucepan. Add the milk, butter and salt and pepper to taste and heat gently until the butter has melted.

Drain the cooked potatoes, then mash in the saucepan until smooth. Pour in the garlic mixture and heat gently, stirring, until the ingredients are combined. Serve hot.

WHEN ROASTED, GARLIC LOSES ITS PUNGENT ACIDITY AND ACQUIRES A DELICIOUS, FULL-FLAVOURED SWEETNESS. SO ALTHOUGH USING TWO WHOLE BULBS MAY SEEM EXCESSIVE, YOU WILL BE SURPRISED AT THE UNIQUELY MELLOW FLAVOUR. IN ADDITION, ROASTED GARLIC LEAVES VERY LITTLE TRACE OF ITS SMELL ON THE BREATH.

CHILLI ROAST POTATOES

SERVES 4

500 g/1 lb 2 oz small new potatoes, scrubbed

150 ml/5 fl oz vegetable oil

1 tsp chilli powder

1/2 tsp caraway seeds

1 tsp salt

Preheat the oven to 200°C/400°F/Gas Mark 6. Cook the potatoes in a large saucepan of boiling water for 10 minutes, then drain thoroughly.

Meanwhile, pour a little of the oil into a shallow roasting tin to coat the base. Heat the oil in the oven for 10 minutes, then remove the tin from the oven. Add the potatoes and brush them with the hot oil.

Mix the chilli powder, caraway seeds and salt together in a small bowl, then sprinkle the mixture evenly over the potatoes, turning them to coat. Add the remaining oil to the tin and return to the oven to roast for 15 minutes, or until the potatoes are cooked through and golden brown.

Using a slotted spoon, remove the potatoes from the tin, draining well, transfer to a large warmed serving dish and serve immediately.

FOR THIS DELICIOUS SIDE DISH, SMALL NEW POTATOES ARE SCRUBBED AND BOILED IN THEIR SKINS, BEFORE BEING COATED IN A HOT CHILLI MIXTURE AND ROASTED TO PERFECTION IN THE OVEN.

ROASTED ROOT VEGETABLES

SERVES 4–6

3 parsnips, cut into
5-cm/2-inch chunks

4 baby turnips, quartered

3 carrots, cut into
5-cm/2-inch chunks

450 g/1 lb butternut
squash, peeled and cut
into 5-cm/2-inch chunks

450 g/1 lb sweet potatoes,
peeled and cut into
5-cm/2-inch chunks

2 garlic cloves,
finely chopped

2 tbsp chopped
fresh rosemary

2 tbsp chopped
fresh thyme

2 tsp chopped fresh sage

3 tbsp olive oil

salt and pepper

2 tbsp chopped fresh
mixed herbs, such as
parsley, thyme and mint,
to garnish

Preheat the oven to 220°C/425°F/Gas Mark 7.

Arrange all the vegetables in a single layer in a large roasting tin. Scatter over the garlic and the herbs. Pour over the oil and season well with salt and pepper.

Toss all the ingredients together until they are well mixed and coated with the oil (you can leave them to marinate at this stage to allow the flavours to be absorbed).

Roast the vegetables at the top of the oven for 50–60 minutes until they are cooked and nicely browned. Turn the vegetables over halfway through the cooking time.

Serve with a good handful of fresh herbs scattered on top and a final sprinkling of salt and pepper to taste.

ROOT VEGETABLES ARE OUR WINTER STAPLES. ROASTED ROOT VEGETABLES ARE PARTICULARLY POPULAR SINCE THEY ALL COOK TOGETHER AND NEED LITTLE ATTENTION ONCE PREPARED. YOU CAN USE WHATEVER IS AVAILABLE: POTATOES, PARSNIPS, TURNIPS, SWEDES, CARROTS AND, ALTHOUGH NOT STRICTLY ROOT VEGETABLES, SQUASH AND ONIONS. SHALLOTS OR WEDGES OF RED ONION ADD EXTRA COLOUR, FLAVOUR AND TEXTURE, AND WHOLE, UNPEELED GARLIC CLOVES ARE ALSO A TASTY ADDITION. TRY TO HAVE ALL THE VEGETABLES CUT TO ROUGHLY THE SAME SIZE. IT'S ALWAYS A GOOD IDEA TO USE A GENEROUS HANDFUL OF HERBS, PARTICULARLY A MIXTURE OF THE STRONGER-FLAVOURED AND MOST AROMATIC ONES, SUCH AS ROSEMARY, THYME AND SAGE.

ROAST SUMMER VEGETABLES

SERVES 4

2 tbsp olive oil

1 fennel bulb

2 red onions

2 beef tomatoes

1 aubergine

2 courgettes

1 yellow pepper

1 red pepper

1 orange pepper

4 garlic cloves, peeled but left whole

4 fresh rosemary sprigs

pepper

crusty bread, to serve (optional)

Preheat the oven to 200°C/400°F/Gas Mark 6.

Brush a large ovenproof dish with a little of the oil. Prepare the vegetables. Cut the fennel bulb, red onions and tomatoes into wedges. Slice the aubergine and courgettes thickly, then deseed all the peppers and cut into chunks. Arrange the vegetables in the dish and tuck the garlic cloves and rosemary sprigs among them. Drizzle with the remaining oil and season to taste with pepper.

Roast the vegetables in the oven for 10 minutes. Remove the dish from the oven and turn the vegetables over using a slotted spoon. Return the dish to the oven and roast for a further 10–15 minutes, or until the vegetables are tender and beginning to turn golden brown.

Serve the vegetables straight from the dish or transfer them to a warmed serving plate. For a vegetarian main course, serve with crusty bread, if you like.

THIS APPETIZING AND COLOURFUL MIXTURE OF MEDITERRANEAN VEGETABLES MAKES A SENSATIONAL SUMMER LUNCH FOR VEGETARIANS AND MEAT-EATERS ALIKE. ROASTING BRINGS OUT THE FULL FLAVOUR AND SWEETNESS OF THE PEPPERS, AUBERGINES, COURGETTES AND ONIONS.

ROASTED ONIONS

SERVES 4

8 large onions, peeled but
left whole

3 tbsp olive oil

55 g/2 oz butter

2 tsp chopped
fresh thyme

200 g/7 oz Cheddar or
Lancashire cheese, grated

salt and pepper

To serve

salad

warm crusty bread

Preheat the oven to 180°C/350°F/Gas Mark 4.

Cut a cross down through the top of each onion towards the root, without cutting all the way through. Place the onions in a roasting tin and drizzle over the oil.

Press a little of the butter into the open crosses, sprinkle with the thyme and season to taste with salt and pepper. Cover with foil and roast in the oven for 40–45 minutes.

Remove the tin from the oven, take off and discard the foil and baste the onions with the pan juices. Return to the oven and cook for a further 15 minutes, uncovered, to allow the onions to brown.

Take the onions out of the oven and scatter the grated cheese over them. Return them to the oven for a few minutes so that the cheese starts to melt.

Serve immediately with some salad and lots of warm crusty bread.

FOR STUFFED ONIONS, BOIL 4 PEELED ONIONS IN SALTED WATER FOR 20 MINUTES. SCOOP OUT THE CENTRES WITH A TEASPOON AND STUFF WITH A MIXTURE OF 55 G/2 OZ GRATED CHEESE, 55 G/2 OZ BREADCRUMBS AND 1 TEASPOON MUSTARD. PLACE THE ONIONS IN AN OVENPROOF DISH, DOT WITH 25 G/1 OZ BUTTER AND ROAST IN A PREHEATED OVEN, 220°C/425°F/GAS MARK 7, FOR 25–30 MINUTES. SERVE HOT AS A STARTER OR AS AN ACCOMPANIMENT TO ROAST MEAT.

OVEN-DRIED TOMATOES

**MAKES 1 X 250-ML/
9-FL OZ JAR**

1 kg/2 lb 4 oz large, juicy,
full-flavoured tomatoes

extra virgin olive oil

sea salt

Preheat the oven to 120°C/250°F/Gas Mark ¹/₂.

Using a sharp knife, cut each of the tomatoes into quarters.

Using a teaspoon, scoop out the seeds and discard. If the tomatoes are large, cut each quarter in half lengthways again.

Sprinkle sea salt in a roasting tin and arrange the tomato slices, skin-side down, on top. Roast in the oven for 2¹/₂ hours, or until the edges are just starting to look charred and the flesh is dry, but still pliable. The exact roasting time and yield will depend on the size and juiciness of the tomatoes. Check the tomatoes at 30-minute intervals after 1¹/₂ hours.

Remove the dried tomatoes from the roasting tin and leave to cool completely. Put in a 250-ml/9-fl oz preserving jar and pour over enough oil to cover. Seal the jar tightly and store in the refrigerator, where the tomatoes will keep for up to 2 weeks.

SERVE THESE OVEN-
DRIED TOMATOES WITH
SLICES OF BUFFALO
MOZZARELLA – DRIZZLE
WITH OLIVE OIL AND
SPRINKLE WITH
COARSELY GROUND
PEPPER AND FINELY
TORN BASIL LEAVES.

CRISPY ROAST ASPARAGUS

SERVES 4

450 g/1 lb asparagus
spears

2 tbsp extra virgin
olive oil

1 tsp coarse sea salt

1 tbsp freshly grated
Parmesan cheese, to serve

Preheat the oven to 200°C/400°F/Gas Mark 6.

Choose asparagus spears of similar widths.
Trim the base of the spears so that all the stems
are approximately the same length.

Arrange the asparagus in a single layer on a
baking sheet. Drizzle with the oil and sprinkle
with the salt.

Place the baking sheet in the oven and roast
the asparagus for 10–15 minutes, turning the
spears once. Remove from the oven and transfer
to a warmed dish. Serve immediately, sprinkled
with grated Parmesan cheese.

As well as there being
both green and white
varieties of asparagus,
there is considerable
variation in width,
so it is important to
try to find spears of a
similar size. Otherwise,
some will be tender
while others require
further cooking. As
a general rule, the
stems of green
asparagus rarely need
peeling, but those of
white asparagus do.

CRISPY ROASTED FENNEL

SERVES 4–6

3 large fennel bulbs

4 tbsp olive oil

juice and finely grated rind
of 1 small lemon

1 garlic clove,
finely chopped

55 g/2 oz fresh white
breadcrumbs

salt and pepper

Preheat the oven to 200°C/400°F/Gas Mark 6.

Trim the fennel bulbs, reserving the green feathery fronds, and cut into quarters. Cook the bulbs in a large saucepan of boiling salted water for 5 minutes until just tender, then drain well.

Heat half the oil in a small roasting tin or flameproof dish, add the fennel and turn to coat in the oil. Drizzle over the lemon juice.

Roast the fennel in the oven for 35 minutes, or until beginning to brown.

Meanwhile, heat the remaining oil in a frying pan. Add the garlic and fry for 1 minute until lightly browned. Add the breadcrumbs and fry, stirring frequently, for 5 minutes, or until crispy. Remove from the heat and stir in the lemon rind, reserved snipped fennel fronds and salt and pepper to taste.

When the fennel is cooked, sprinkle the breadcrumb mixture over the top and return to the oven for a further 5 minutes. Serve hot.

IT IS SAID THAT MALE FENNEL HAS MORE FLAVOUR THAN FEMALE FENNEL. TO DISTINGUISH ONE FROM THE OTHER, THE MALE IS LONG AND THIN, WHILE THE FEMALE IS BULBOUS, AS THOUGH IT HAS HIPS.

ROAST LEEKS

SERVES 6

4 leeks

3 tbsp olive oil

2 tsp balsamic vinegar

sea salt and pepper

IF IN SEASON, 8 BABY LEEKS MAY BE USED INSTEAD OF THE STANDARD-SIZED ONES. SHERRY VINEGAR MAKES A GOOD SUBSTITUTE FOR THE EXPENSIVE BALSAMIC VINEGAR AND WOULD WORK AS WELL IN THIS RECIPE.

Preheat the oven to 200°C/400°F/Gas Mark 6.

Halve the leeks lengthways, making sure that your knife cuts straight, so that the leek is held together by the root. Rinse thoroughly, fanning the layers gently, under cold running water to remove all traces of soil and grit. Pat dry with kitchen paper.

Place the leeks in a single layer in a roasting tin and brush with the oil. Roast in the oven for 20–30 minutes until tender and just beginning to colour.

Remove the leeks from the oven and brush with balsamic vinegar. Sprinkle with salt and pepper to taste and serve hot or warm.

INDEX

apple sauce 26
apricot sauce 38
asparagus 91
aubergine 60, 84

beef
  cuts 9
  pot roast, with potatoes and dill 12
  roast beef 10
beurre manié 12
brandy sauce 50

cabbage 46
carrots 83
chicken
  poussins, with herbs and wine 34
  roast 32
cider sauce 42
cod
  Italian 69
  roasted with lime 72
courgettes 84
crackling 26
Cumberland sauce 22

duckling, boned and stuffed 38

equipment 7, 9

fennel 66, 84, 92
fish 52–73
  cod 69, 72
  fillets 57, 64, 69, 72
  haddock 64
  mackerel 70
  monkfish 63
  salmon 57
  sea bass 54, 72
  sea bream 66
  tuna 58

game
  guinea fowl 31, 46
  pheasant 31, 45
  quail 31, 48
  venison 31, 50
gammon 22
garlic, roast 78, 83, 84
goose, with honey and pears 37

guinea fowl, with cabbage 46

haddock, garlic-crusted 64
ham 22, 63

lamb
  cuts 9
  leg, pot roasted 17
  with orzo 18
  rack of 14
  with rosemary and Marsala 21
lardons 46
leeks 94

mackerel, Mediterranean-style 70
meat 8–29
  beef 10–13
  lamb 14–21
  pork 22–9
  resting after cooking 7
mint sauce 14
monkfish, with Romesco sauce 63

onion
  roast 83, 84, 86
  stuffed 86
orzo 18

parsnips 83
peppers 28, 63, 84
pheasant, with red wine and
  herbs 45
plaice, roasted with lime 72
pork
  cuts 9
  gammon 22
  lardons 46
  loin
    with crackling 26
    slow-roasted 25
  shoulder, with sweet peppers 28
port and cranberry sauce 40
pot roast
  beef 12
  lamb 17
potatoes
  mashed 64, 78
  pancake 48
  roast 17, 37, 76, 80

poultry
  chicken 31, 32–5
  duckling 31, 38
  goose 31, 37
  turkey 31, 40–3
poussins, with herbs and wine 34

quail, with grapes 48

Romesco sauce 63

salmon, with lemon and herbs 57
sauce
  apple 26
  apricot 38
  brandy 50
  cider 42
  Cumberland 22
  mint 14
  port and cranberry 40
  Romesco 63
sea bass 54, 72
sea bream, with fennel 66
seafood 53, 60
squash 60, 83
stuffing 38, 40, 42
sweet potato 83

tomatoes 70
  oven-dried 88
  roast 84
tuna, with orange and anchovies 58
turkey
  with cider sauce 42
  with wine and mushrooms 40
turnips 34, 83

vegetables 74–95
  asparagus 91
  fennel 66, 92
  leeks 94
  onions 86
  potatoes 76–81
  roast with seafood 60
  root 83
  spring 34
  summer 84
  tomatoes 84, 88
venison, with brandy sauce 50